Oceanography
The Study of Oceans

SUSAN H. GRAY

Children's Press®
An Imprint of Scholastic Inc.
New York Toronto London Auckland Sydney
Mexico City New Delhi Hong Kong
Danbury, Connecticut

Content Consultant
Dr. Lisa Campbell
Texas A&M University

Library of Congress Cataloging-in-Publication Data
Gray, Susan Heinrichs.
 Oceanography the study of oceans/Susan H. Gray.
     p. cm.—(A true book)
 Includes bibliographical references and index.
 ISBN-13: 978-0-531-24679-5 (lib. bdg.)   ISBN-10: 0-531-24679-5 (lib. bdg.)
 ISBN-13: 978-0-531-28273-1 (pbk.)   ISBN-10: 0-531-28273-2 (pbk.)
 1. Oceanography—Juvenile literature. I. Title. II. Series.
 GC21.5.G737 2012
 551.46—dc23   2011031074

Published in 2012 by Children's Press, an imprint of Scholastic Inc.
Printed in China 62

Find the Truth!

Everything you are about to read is true *except* for one of the sentences on this page.

Which one is **TRUE**?

T or F Most plankton live near the ocean floor.

T or F Pressure increases as you go deeper in the ocean.

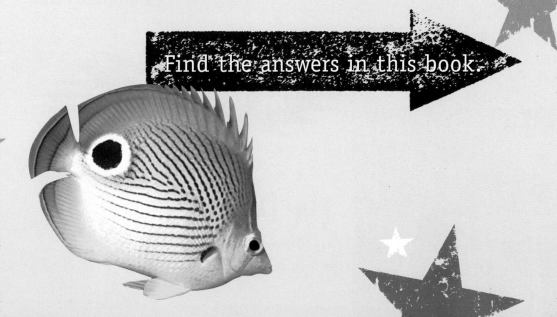

Find the answers in this book.

3

Contents

1 The Science of Oceanography

What do oceanographers do?.................. 7

2 The History of Oceanography

Why did people once fear ocean travel?........ 11

3 The Five Oceans

What have scientists found on
the ocean floor? 17

THE **BIG** TRUTH!

The Deep, Deep Sea

Just how deep can a person go in
the ocean? 26

Some coral reefs support more than 1,300 different kinds of fish.

4 Amazing Sea Life

Why are microscopic plants and animals so important?........................... 31

5 New Discoveries, New Questions

What are oceanographers working on right now?................................... 39

True Statistics........... 43

Resources 44

Important Words........ 46

Index 47

About the Author........ 48

This fish grows no bigger than a child's hand.

5

Feeding a shark can
be a dangerous task.

CHAPTER 1

The Science of Oceanography

Did you know that hot, molten rock is oozing from the seafloor? Have you ever heard that whales sing as they travel? Can you imagine swimming beneath a thick sheet of ice? Do you know about the octopus that pretends it's a snake? If any of these questions interest you, you might want to learn about oceanography. Oceanography is the study of the earth's oceans and seas.

Some divers wear special metal suits to protect themselves when working with dangerous sharks.

Different Views of the Ocean

The people who study the oceans are called oceanographers. Some oceanographers are interested in landforms. They study the features of the seafloor. They look at underwater volcanoes and mountain ranges. They watch scalding hot water spew from holes in the seafloor. They try to figure out how these features change over time.

Some oceanographers use special equipment to create maps of the ocean floor.

Oceanographers often become experts on weather and climate.

Oceanographers use floating buoys to record weather information.

Some oceanographers study the water's movements. They look at how water interacts with the air above it. They work to understand how the oceans affect the weather. Many other oceanographers are interested in plant and animal life. They learn how different **organisms** depend on each other for survival. Some oceanographers keep track of pollution in the ocean. They study how it harms the sea life. They also think of ways to protect the ocean environment from pollution.

Long ago, people often imagined that the oceans were filled with sea monsters like this.

The History of Oceanography

Oceans and seas have fascinated people for centuries. Long ago, people knew little about them. Some people believed a ship could sail to the edge of the earth and tumble off. There were some people who believed that the gods controlled the waves. They offered gifts to these gods to make them happy and to keep the seas calm.

 Artists sometimes got their ideas from sailors who told terrifying stories.

Some Brave Sailors

Most early sailing trips were short. For instance, Greek traders only sailed from island to island. But in 1492, Christopher Columbus sailed from Spain across the Atlantic. After two months, he reached a group of islands near present-day Florida. About 30 years later, Ferdinand Magellan and his crew made an even longer trip. They sailed around the world.

In 1768, England's James Cook led the first scientific **voyage**. Scientists traveled with him to gather information on any new plants and animals they saw.

Magellan died before making it all the way around the world. His crew finished the journey without him.

The *Challenger*'s crew made many important discoveries on its journey.

In 1872, England sent out another group to study "everything about the sea." Sailing aboard the *Challenger*, British scientists visited the Atlantic, Pacific, and Indian Oceans. They discovered thousands of new plants and animals. They measured water temperatures and checked the ocean depths. They took samples from the seafloor. It is considered one of the greatest scientific expeditions of all time.

Groundbreaking Ideas

The years following the *Challenger*'s journey were exciting ones. An American naval officer built a machine that could measure ocean depths. Oceanographers discovered amazing new types of plants and animals. In 1912, German scientist Alfred Wegener introduced his theory of **continental** drift. Wegener claimed that the earth's continents had once been joined as one big supercontinent. Over time, it broke into pieces that drifted apart. They became the continents we know today.

Timeline of Oceanography

1492–1504
Columbus makes several trips across the Atlantic.

1519–1521
Magellan sails around the globe.

1768–1779
Captain James Cook makes three scientific voyages.

Scientists debated Wegener's ideas for decades. Parts of it were proven to be wrong. But his ideas set the stage for future oceanographers.

In the 1950s and 1960s, scientists discovered widening cracks in the sea floor. They found underwater mountain chains. These could only have been caused by movements of the earth's crust. Today, scientists agree that the crust is broken into large, slowly moving plates. These plates collide, scoot apart, and grind against each other. Scientists use the theory of **plate tectonics** to describe these movements.

1872–1876
The British ship *Challenger* makes its voyage.

1912
Alfred Wegener introduces the theory of continental drift.

1960s
Scientists develop the theories of seafloor spreading and plate tectonics.

15

CHAPTER 3

The Five Oceans

Five oceans make up the earth's largest bodies of water. These include the Atlantic, Pacific, Indian, Arctic, and Southern Oceans. The Pacific and Atlantic are divided into northern and southern regions. The Southern Ocean is the most recently named ocean. It was named in 2000 and includes the water surrounding Antarctica.

None of these five oceans is completely surrounded by land. They flow into one another, forming one enormous body of water.

Oceans cover about 71 percent of the earth's surface.

Arctic Ocean

Atlantic
Ocean

Pacific
Ocean

Pacific
Ocean

Indian
Ocean

Southern Ocean

This satellite image shows all five of Earth's oceans.

Salt Everywhere

Oceans contain saltwater. Much of this salt comes from the land. Rainwater runs down mountainsides. It washes across plains and into rivers. The water picks up salt from the ground along the way. Eventually, rivers carry the salt into the ocean. Meanwhile, the sun heats the ocean's surface. This causes the water to evaporate into gas and rises to form clouds. Most of the salt is left behind.

Saltiness, or **salinity**, is measured in parts per thousand, or ppt. Ocean water's salinity is about 35 ppt. This means that every 1,000 pounds (454 kilograms) of seawater contains 35 pounds (16 kg) of salt. This is far too salty for humans to drink. But it does not bother the ocean animals. Their bodies filter out excess salt from the water as it enters their systems.

Ocean animals such as fish are equipped to live in salty water.

Temperature and Pressure

Ocean temperatures cover a wide range. Surface waters in the Arctic and Southern Oceans are icy cold. Surface waters in the southern Pacific and Indian Oceans are quite warm. Rain, wind, and the sun's heat affect the water temperature at the surface. But deeper down, the sun's warmth fades away. Wind and rain have little effect. The water gradually gets colder. At the deep ocean floor, the water is just above freezing.

Sunlight keeps surface waters warm in many parts of the world.

Divers at certain depths use tanks that provide a special mix of gasses for them to breathe.

Divers can damage their bodies by remaining in deep water for too long.

Pressure also increases as you move deeper into the ocean. On land we don't notice it, but the weight of the atmosphere presses down on our bodies. In the ocean, water also presses down. As a diver descends, the amount of water above the diver increases. Therefore, the pressure on his or her body increases. Divers working at extreme depths wear special suits. These are built to protect their bodies.

Most ocean plants grow near the surface, where sunlight is more plentiful.

Sunlight

On land, sunlight falls on mosses, ferns, and trees. Their cells use the sun's energy to change different chemicals into food. This process is called **photosynthesis**. Ocean plants do the same. Sunlight filters through the water, reaching tiny floating plants. Sunlight also shines on strands of seaweed. These plants carry on photosynthesis to live and grow.

Just beneath the ocean's surface, the sunlight is quite bright. In fact, in the upper 330 feet (100 meters) of the water, there is enough light for plants to survive. But as you go deeper, the sunlight dims. It becomes too faint for plants to photosynthesize. The only plants here are dead ones that are sinking down from above. Below about 3,300 feet (1,000 m), the sea becomes completely dark.

The fangtooth lives in complete darkness 3 miles (4.5 km) below the ocean's surface.

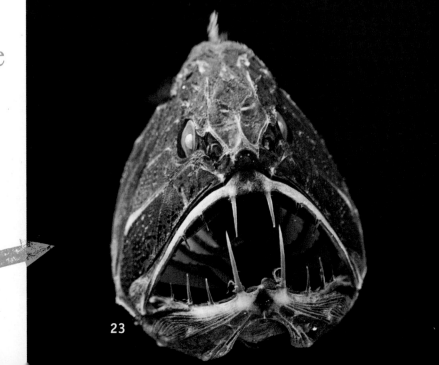

Where Land and Sea Meet

At the edges of the continents, the land gently slopes into the sea. This shallow, sloping region is called the continental shelf. Next, the land drops off and becomes much steeper. This region is called the continental slope. Then the slope levels off a bit into a zone called the continental rise. The rise leads to the deep ocean floor.

On average, the continental shelf extends about 40 miles (60 km) into the ocean.

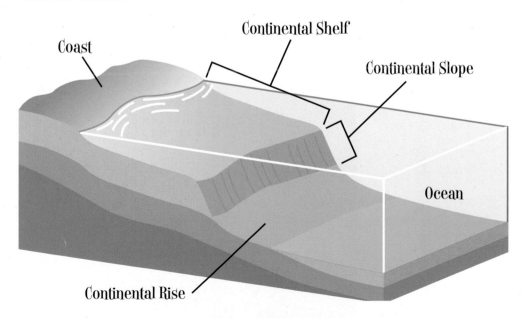

Coast

Continental Shelf

Continental Slope

Ocean

Continental Rise

Surprises on the Ocean Floor

Part of the ocean floor is completely flat. This is called the **abyssal** plain. A chain of volcanic mountains rises from the plain. Some are active, with hot rock and ash flowing from them. Others have been quiet for centuries. Many of these mountains are among the tallest on Earth. Some reach well above water, creating islands.

THE **BIG** TRUTH!

The Deep, Deep Sea

Many oceanographers are fascinated by deep-sea trenches. These are huge cracks in the ocean floor. The Java Trench lies in the Indian Ocean. Its lowest spot is more than 4 miles (6.4 km) down. The Puerto Rico Trench in the Atlantic is even deeper. But the Mariana Trench has the deepest spot known. Lying in the Pacific, it extends almost 7 miles (11.3km) into the earth.

In 1960, the U.S. Navy sent a manned vehicle to the bottom of the Mariana Trench. The navy was testing a special deep-water vessel named *Trieste*. The sphere at the bottom of the vessel housed two men. It had thick steel walls and a single round window.

The two divers inside were Don Walsh (left) and Jacques Piccard. They shared a small, cramped space inside the cabin. As the *Trieste* descended, the cabin grew cold. The men had to put on warmer clothing. They ate candy bars during the trip to keep up their energy.

It took almost five hours to reach the bottom of the trench. Walsh and Piccard switched on some high-powered lights and looked outside. They were surprised to see shrimp and fish. The men spent about 20 minutes at the bottom before returning to the surface.

On the Go

The ocean is never still. At the surface, waves are whipped along by the wind. On quiet or breezy days, the waves are low and calm. But during storms, the winds stir up huge, violent waves. Some of the most powerful waves occur right after underwater earthquakes. These deep-sea jolts are such a shock that they can produce waves hundreds of feet tall. These waves are called **tsunamis**.

Tsunamis can cause serious damage to towns along ocean coasts.

Tides are caused by the gravity of the sun and the moon pulling on the water.

Tides are slow movements of the entire ocean. They are seen along any shoreline. The water takes hours to creep up the shore. Then it takes hours for the water level to fall again.

Currents are "rivers in the ocean." They are areas where the water flows in a specific direction. The wind and the earth's spin are two things that can produce currents.

The mimic octopus moves its tentacles to make itself look like other animals.

CHAPTER **4**

Amazing Sea Life

The oceans are home to some of the most unusual organisms on the earth. Some algae have tiny, air-filled balloons that help them float near the water's surface. The mimic octopus pretends to be a sea snake, a poisonous fish, or a jellyfish to escape danger.

The blobfish floats above the sea floor waiting for slow-moving prey to drift by. And the clownfish finds safety among poisonous sea anemones. All sea creatures depend on one another for food or protection.

Many octopuses can change colors.

Small but Important

The upper layers of the ocean receive the most sunlight. Billions of microscopic plants and animals live in this region. These organisms, called plankton, depend on water movements to wash them around. The tiny plants use the sun's energy to produce food. The animals feed on other plankton that drift by. Although these organisms are smaller than pinheads, they are quite important to ocean life.

Plankton are just the right size for newly hatched fish to eat.

The plankton in this photograph are magnified several times.

Humpback whales eat huge amounts of plankton.

Very young fish feed almost entirely on animal plankton. They dart after these weak swimmers and swallow them whole. Some fish continue to eat plankton as adults. Humpback whales eat plankton that they filter from the water. Sponges and tube-dwelling worms also eat plankton. So do the tiny animals that build coral **reefs**. Without plankton, many sea creatures would not survive.

It is difficult to spot a well-hidden leafy sea dragon.

Eat or Be Eaten

Eating is only one thing animals do to survive. Another is to keep from being eaten! To avoid becoming another animal's meal, many animals use **camouflage**. Camouflaged animals have unusual colors, patterns, or limbs. These help them blend in with their surroundings. The leafy sea dragon is one such fish. It appears to have stems and leaves growing from its body. **Predators** see this "plant" and pass right by.

Sea slugs use warning colors. These soft-bodied, slow-moving animals are easy targets. But their bright, shocking colors tell predators that they are poisonous and to keep away.

Many butterfly fish fool their enemies another way. These fish have a large black spot near the tail. The spot looks a lot like an eye. Predators snap at that spot, hoping to bite the fish's head. Instead, they get a mouthful of water as the fish shoots away.

Most butterfly fish have bright colors.

Predators have a hard time telling the butterfly fish's head from its tail.

Sea animals are built for ocean life. Whales, for example, must breathe air before they dive for food. However, many whales can hold their breath underwater for more than an hour. Crabs often lose their legs to predators. But they can grow them back later. Jellyfish cannot chase after food. But they can sting and paralyze fish that wander by. Seals have extra body fat to insulate them, keeping them warm in icy waters.

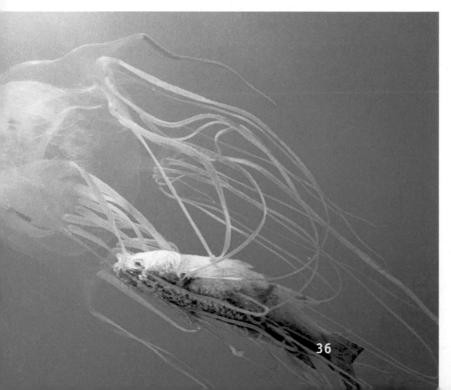

Jellyfish use their tentacles to paralyze unlucky fish that swim nearby.

Living Lights

What do animals in the deepest, darkest waters do if they need light? They make their own! This is known as **bioluminescence**. The bodies of bioluminescent animals contain a special chemical. It combines with oxygen to produce light like the blue in the comb jelly below. Some animals flash their lights to attract mates. Others use them to catch prey. The anglerfish dangles a lighted organ from its head. Smaller fish come to check it out and are quickly swallowed.

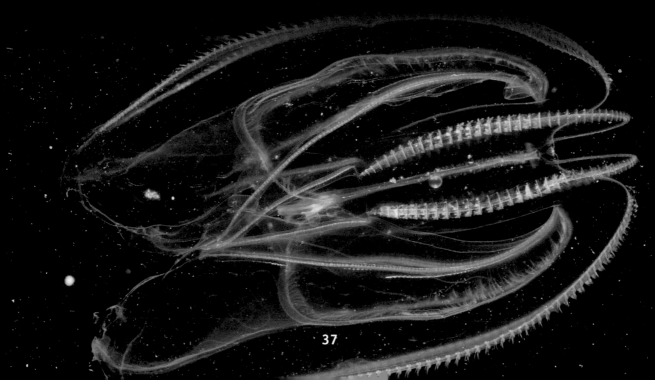

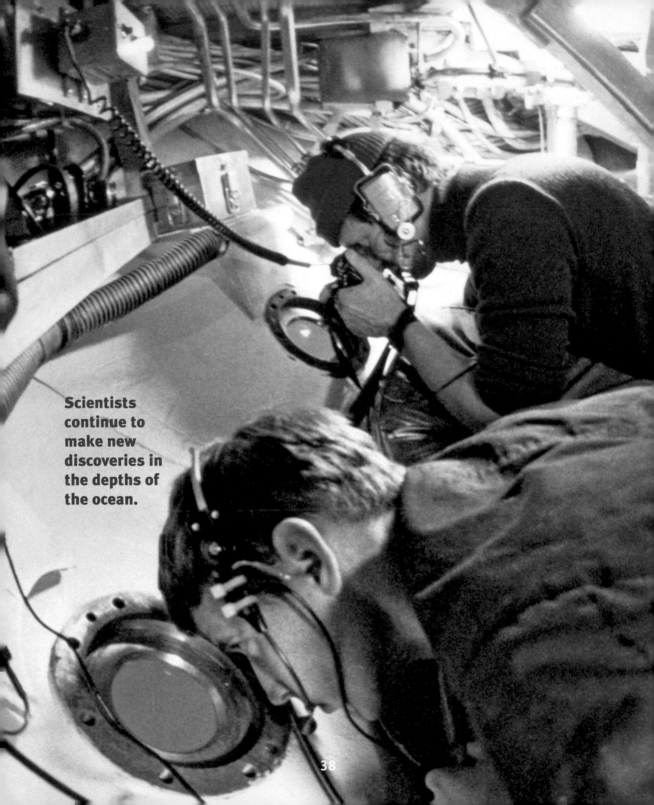

Scientists continue to make new discoveries in the depths of the ocean.

CHAPTER 5

New Discoveries, New Questions

Scientists are constantly working to learn more about the oceans. Some are looking at the deep seafloor. They have discovered hot springs there. The water bubbles up from deep inside the earth. Amazingly, giant clams, spider crabs, and tubeworms live nearby. Some scientists are learning how these organisms can stand such heat and what they eat. Other scientists are building better equipment for studying this unusual environment.

This submarine's windows are built to withstand great pressure.

Finding Ways to Help

Some oceanographers study pollution in the ocean. Scientists find scraps of plastic in fish stomachs. These scraps also appear in birds that eat the fish. The plastic in the ocean comes from careless humans. When people litter, the trash is often carried to the ocean. Sometimes, people dump their trash directly into the ocean. This harms ocean life. Scientists work to stop such pollution. They hope to protect the plants and animals that live in the sea.

Even huge animals such as whales can get caught in trash and fishing nets.

Scientists work together to share their findings and come up with new ideas.

Many oceanographers are learning more about ocean animals. One group is studying camouflage in the cuttlefish. The cuttlefish is a relative of the octopus. It has millions of color-changing cells in its skin. The cells are constantly changing to match its surroundings. Scientists hope to understand how the cuttlefish does this. This might help them improve camouflage for soldiers in battle.

Many students study oceanography in college.

A Big Job

Only 10 percent of the earth's oceans have been explored. More than 200,000 different organisms have been named. But scientists believe that as many as 2,000,000 kinds of organisms make the oceans their home. There is a lot about the ocean that is still to be discovered. Each new discovery uncovers new questions. Will you be the one to answer them one day? ★

True Statistics

Pressure at the bottom of the Mariana Trench: More than 16,000 lbs. per sq. in. (1,125 kg per sq cm)

Salinity of the earth's oceans: Between 32 and 37 parts per thousand

Distance sailed by the ship *Challenger*: 68,890 nautical mi. (127,600 km)

Number of new plants and animals discovered during *Challenger*'s exploration: 4,717

Largest ocean animal: The blue whale, which weighs around 150 tons (136 metric tons)

Highest tides in the world: At the Bay of Fundy in Canada, where high tide can be more than 53 feet (16 m) above low tide

Greatest volcanic activity on the earth: Underwater, where about 90 percent of all active volcanoes are

Did you find the truth?

F Most plankton live near the ocean floor.

T Pressure increases as you go deeper in the ocean.

Resources

Books

Berkenkamp, Lauri. *Discover the Oceans: The World's Largest Ecosystem*. White River Junction, VT: Nomad Press, 2009.

Bingham, Jane. *Captain Cook's Pacific Explorations*. Chicago: Heinemann-Raintree, 2007.

Ganeri, Anita. *Ocean Divers*. Chicago: Heinemann-Raintree, 2011.

McMillan, Beverly, and John A. Musick. *Oceans*. New York: Simon & Schuster Children's Publishing, 2007.

Moore, Heidi. *Ocean Food Chains*. Chicago: Heinemann-Raintree, 2010.

Pedersen, Traci Steckel. *Oceanography*. Logan, IA: Perfection Learning, 2007.

Stiefel, Chana. *Tsunamis*. New York: Children's Press, 2009.

Woods, Michael, and Mary B. Woods. *Seven Natural Wonders of the Arctic, Antarctica, and the Oceans*. Minneapolis: Twenty-First Century Books, 2009.

Organizations and Web Sites

Kids.gov: Earth Science—Oceanography

www.kids.gov/6_8/6_8_science_oceanography.shtml
This site has links to pages covering shipwrecks, marine animals, underwater photographs, and much more.

Year of the Ocean—Kids' and Teachers' Corner

www.yoto98.noaa.gov/kids.htm
This site has fun learning activities, fact sheets on ocean species, and things you can do to save coral reefs.

Places to Visit

Aquarium of the Pacific

100 Aquarium Way
Long Beach, CA 90802
(562) 590-3100
www.aquariumofpacific.org
See the shark lagoon, take one of the behind-the-scenes tours, or visit the forest of colorful Australian birds.

John G. Shedd Aquarium

1200 South Lake Shore Drive
Chicago, IL 60605
(312) 939-2438
www.sheddaquarium.org
This aquarium includes examples of different habitats and a kids' activity center.

Visit this Scholastic web site for more information on oceanography:

www.factsfornow.scholastic.com

Important Words

abyssal (uh-BISS-uhl) — having to do with the bottom waters of the ocean

bioluminescence (by-o-loo-mih-NESS-uhnts) — production of light by living organisms

camouflage (KAM-uh-flahzh) — coloring or covering that makes animals, people, and objects blend in with their surroundings

continental (kon-tuh-NIN-tuhl) — relating to the earth's large landmasses

organisms (OR-guh-nih-zumz) — living plants or animals

photosynthesis (foe-toe-SIN-thuh-sihss) — a chemical process by which green plants make their food

plate tectonics (PLAYT tek-TAHN-iks) — the theory that the earth's crust is divided into several large plates

predators (PRED-uh-turz) — animals that live by hunting other animals for food

reefs (REEFS) — strips of rock, sand, or coral close to the surface of the ocean or another body of water

salinity (suh-LIH-nih-tee) — saltiness

tsunamis (tsu-NAH-meez) — waves caused by an underwater earthquake or volcano

voyage (VOI-ij) — a long journey by sea or in space

Index

Page numbers in **bold** indicate illustrations

algae, 31
animals, **6**, 7, 9, 12, 13, 14, **19**, **23**, 27, **30**, 31, **32**, **33**, **34–36**, **37**, 39, **40**, 41, 42
Arctic Ocean, 17, 20
Atlantic Ocean, 12, 13, 14, 17, 26

bioluminescence, **37**

camouflage, **30**, 31, **34**, **35**, 41
Challenger (ship), **13**, 15
clams, 39
clownfish, 31
colors, 31, 35, 41
comb jellies, **37**
continental drift, 14–15
continental slope, 24
coral reefs, 33
crabs, 36, 39
currents, 29

deep-water vessels, **27**, **38**, 39
depths, 13, 14, **21**
divers, **6**, 7, **21**, **27**

humpback whales, **33**

Indian Ocean, 13, 17, 20, 26

Java Trench, 26
jellyfish, **36**

leafy sea dragons, **34**

maps, **8**
Mariana Trench, 26–27
mimic octopuses, **30**, 31
mountains, 8, 15, 18, 25

ocean floor, 8, 13, 15, 20, 24, 25, 26, 31, 39
oceanographers, **8–9**, 12, **13**, 14, 15, 26, **38**, 39, 40, **41**, 42
octopuses, **30**, 31, 41
organisms. *See* animals; plants.

Pacific Ocean, 13, 17, 20, 26
photosynthesis, 22, 23
plankton, **32–33**
plants, 9, 12, 13, 14, **22**, 23, 32, 40, 42
plate tectonics, 15
pollution, 9, **40**
pressure, 21, 39
Puerto Rico Trench, 26

sailing, 11, 12–13, **14**, 15
saltwater, 18–**19**
sea anemones, 31
seals, 36
sharks, **6**, 7
Southern Ocean, 17, 20
sponges, 33
sunlight, 18, **20**, **22–23**, 32

temperatures, 13, **20**, 27
tides, **29**
timeline, **14–15**
tools, **9**, **21**, **27**, **38**, 39
trenches, 26–27
Trieste (deep-water vessel), **27**
tsunamis, **28**
tubeworms, 33, 39

volcanoes, 8, **25**

waves, 11, 28
weather, **9**, 20, 28
whales, **33**, 36, **40**

About the Author

Susan H. Gray has a master's degree in zoology and has also studied geology and paleontology. She has written more than 120 reference books for children. Susan especially likes to write on topics that engage children in science. She and her husband, Michael, live in Cabot, Arkansas.